Memorandum

von .... | an ....

, den .... 19......

GIRL
I KEEP
THINKING OF
YOU

AF631947

FAVORIT

Memorandum

von .... an ....

....

...., den..19........

IT FEELS
LIKE DOING
HOME WORKS
BUT IT'S
LIVING

FAVORIT

Memorandum

von .... an ....

....

........................, den .... 19......

I WANT
TO WRITE
YOU
SOMETHING
SUPER ROMANTIC
BUT

FAVORIT

Memorandum

von .... an ....

....

...., den..19........

I WONDER
WHAT WILL
MAKE ME
HAPPY THIS
WEEK
CAUSE
YOUR EYES
LOST THEIR
SHINE
BABY GIRL

FAVORIT

Memorandum

von .... an ....

.... , den .... 19......

ON THE DATE
WE NEVER
HAD YOU
LOOKED AMAZING
& WE WEREN'T
SHY

FAVORIT

Memorandum

von .... an ....

.... , den .... 19......

I WENT
SUPERFAR
AWAY BABY
BUT STILL
SAW YOU
WALKING AROUND
EVERYWHERE.
EVERY CORNER
IS MADE OF US.

FAVORIT

Memorandum

von .... | an ....

...., den .... 19......

EVERY WORD
IS MADE
OF YOU
BABY GIRL

FAVORIT

Memorandum

von .... an ....

....

..................., den .... 19........

AMERICAN BREAKFAST
IN SEOUL.
COFFEE SUCKS
BABY GIRL
BUT YOU WAINTING
4 ME IN THE FUTURE
SO I'M GONNA PICK U
UP AND I'LL TAKE YOU
WITH CAUSE WE SUPER
WORTH IT ♡

Memorandum

von .... | an ....

...., den .... 19........

AFTER ALL
THE WRITING
COMES THE
TOUCHING
AND I WILL
NEVER STOP
WRITING YOU
BABY GIRL
AND I WILL NEVER
STOP TOUCHING YOU
BABY GIRL

FAVORIT

Memorandum

von .... an ....

....

...., den .... 19....

BABY GIRL
LOOKING 4
WORDS BUT
MY BRAIN IS
KIND OF EMPTY
AND THE BIGGEST
POEM IS THAT
I WANNA SEE
YOU. SO SIMPLE
IT IS.

FAVORIT

Memorandum

von .... an ....

....

........................, den .... 19....

NEVER HIGH
NEVER LIE
SMILE ME
THLOUGH
THE DAY
YOU BANG
ME AND I
STAY. GIRL
YOU IS THE
SWEETEST ~~[illegible]~~ DAY

FAVORIT

Memorandum

von .... an ....

....

................................., den ....19.......

STILL
NOT MUCH
TO SAY

FAVORIT

Memorandum

von .... an ....

....

............, den .... 19....

NORMAL BODIES
BABY GIRL
CAUSE THERE'S
NO SIX PACK HERE
AROUND
REAL LIKE REAL
LIFE BABY
WE MAYBE COULD
MAKE EACH OTHER
GIRL

FAVORIT

Memorandum

von .... an ....

...., den .... 19...

YOU USED TO
GIVE ME LIKES
AND I WAS
HAPPY. YOU
CALLED ME
BABY GIRL
AND I WAS
HAPPY. ONLINE
4EVER BUT WE
MET NEVER
TOUCHING MYSELF VERY DEEP IN THE HEART.

FAVORIT

Memorandum

von .... an ....

...., den .... 19....

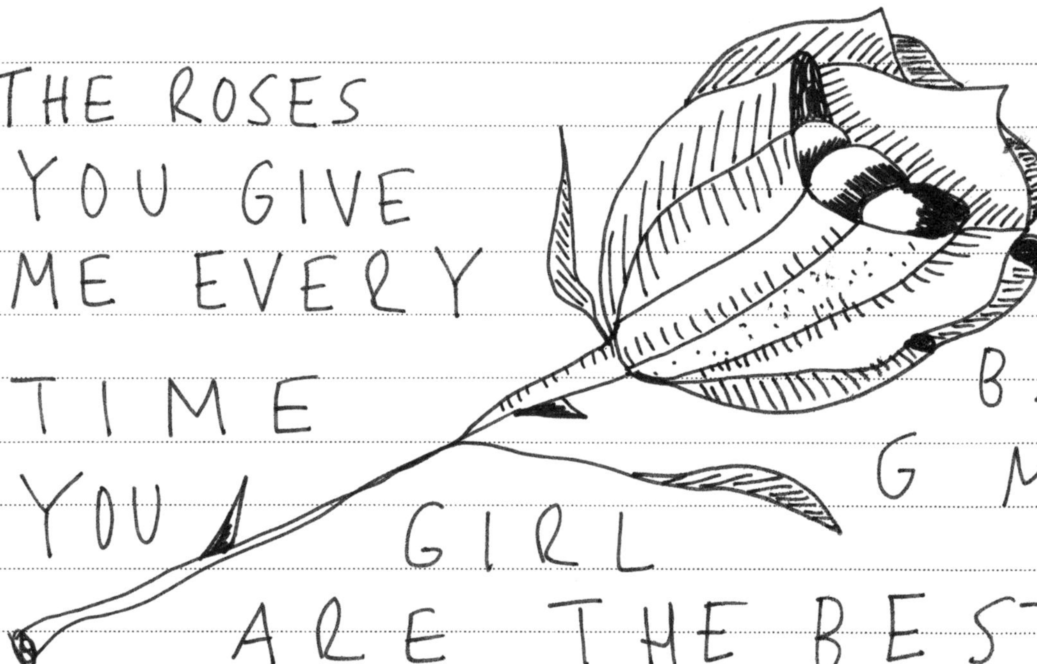

THE ROSES
YOU GIVE
ME EVERY
TIME
YOU
GIRL
ARE THE BEST

BAN
G ME

FAVORIT

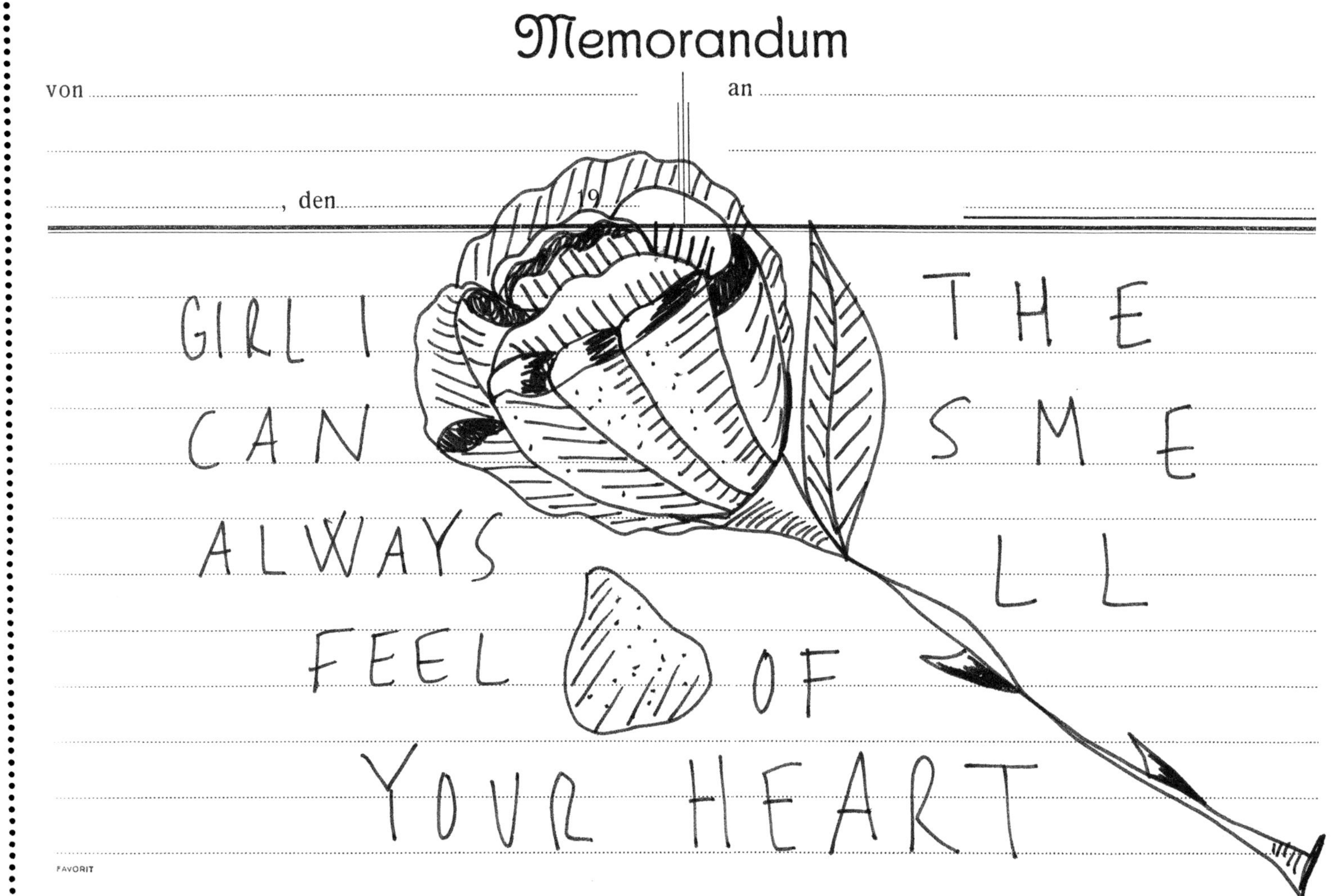
Memorandum
von
an
, den
19
GIRL I
CAN
ALWAYS
FEEL
THE
SME
LL
OF
YOUR HEART
FAVORIT

Memorandum

von ....

....

........................, den .... 19......

an ....

GIRL

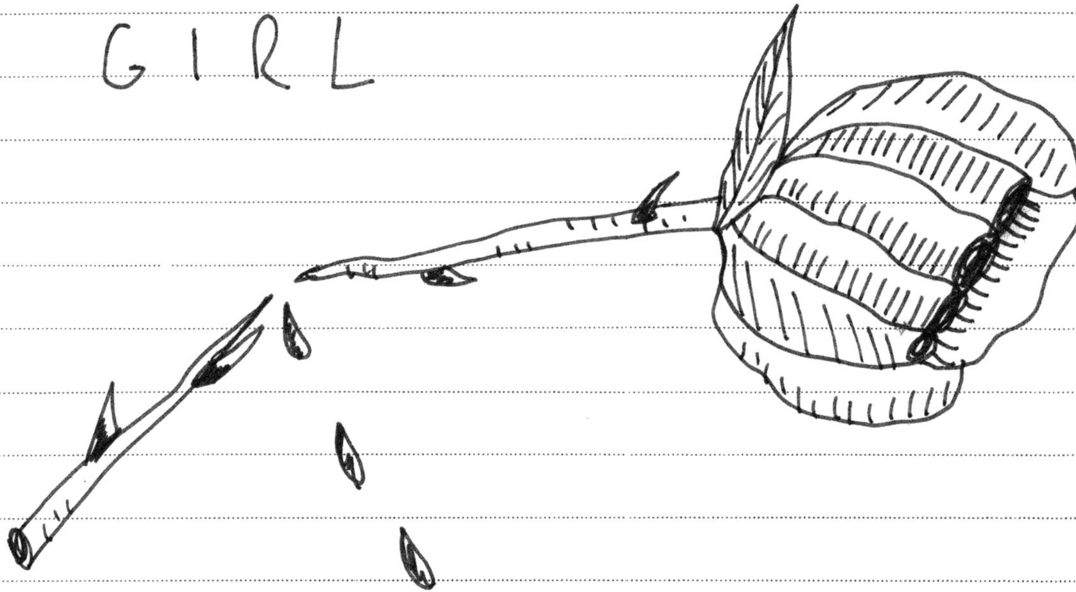

Memorandum

von …… an ……

……, den …… 19……

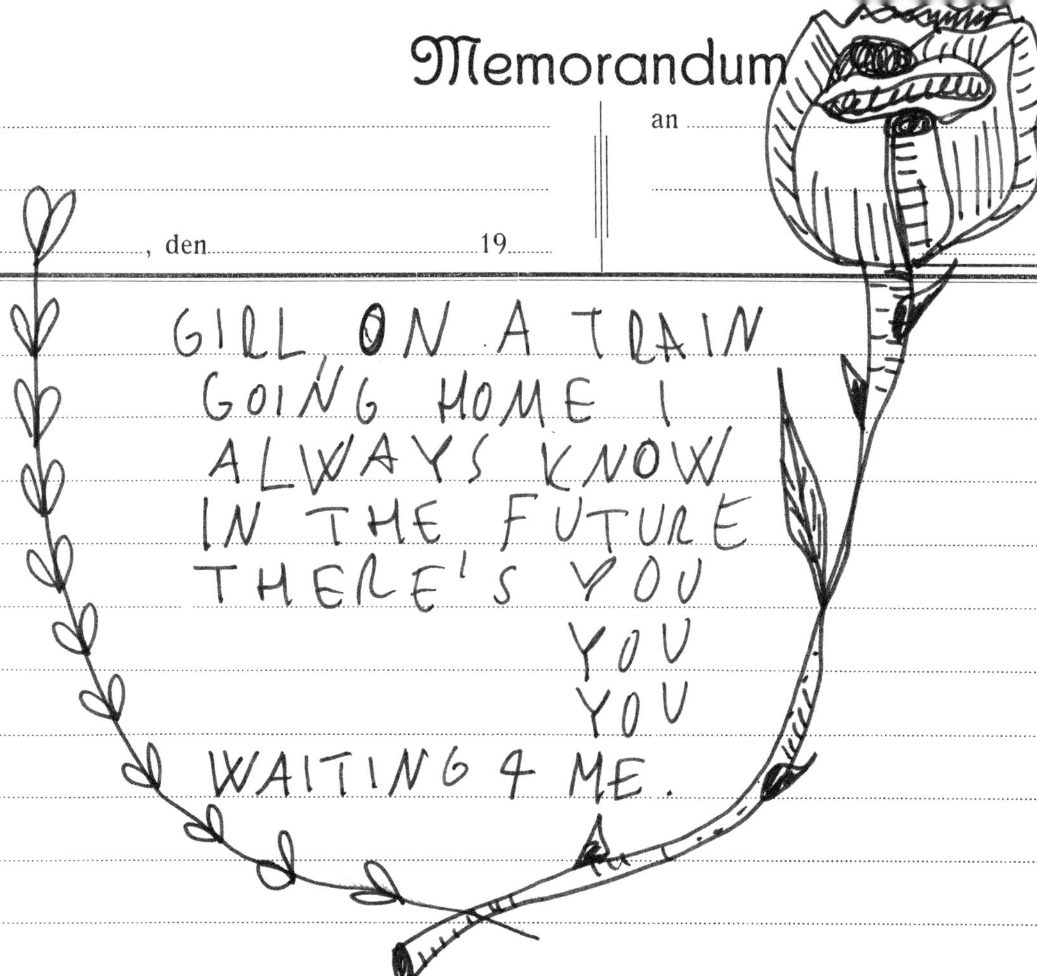

GIRL ON A TRAIN
GOING HOME I
ALWAYS KNOW
IN THE FUTURE
THERE'S YOU
YOU
YOU
WAITING 4 ME.

FAVORIT

Memorandum

von

, den 19

an

I'M YOUR
WIFEY

BABY
GIRL

FAVORIT

Memorandum

von .... | an ....

....

...., den .... 19......

I'M YOUR WORLD
VISION GIRL
YOU TOUCH ME
DEEP AND I LICK
LICK LICK IT.
I GIVE IT 2YOU
HARD YOU GIVE
IT BACK 2ME.
LET'S KEEP
SPACE AND TIME
26ETHER

FAVORIT

Memorandum

von .... an ....

...., den .... 19.......

BABY YOU'RE
THE
BANG IN MY
HEART

AND YOU
GROW
GROW
GROW

FAVORIT

Memorandum

von .... | an ....

...., den .... 19......

AND WE
GROW
GROW
GROW
BABYGIRL
SO
FUCK
THE
REST

FAVORIT

Memorandum

von .... an ....

....

...., den..19........

TAKING A
FLIGHT
THAT IS
NOT GOING
YOUR DIRECTION
GIRL.
YOU 4 SURE
KNOW
FUCK
IS WHAT
WE WANNA DO.

FAVORIT

Memorandum

von ....

....

.............................., den .... 19......

an ....

WE SHOULD
STICK
2GETHER
AT LEAST
VERY
SWEATY
ALL THE
NIGHT
IN MY
BED

FAVORIT

Memorandum

von ....

.... , den .... 19......

an ....

GIRL
YOU'R
THE
POEM
I WANT
TO
WAKE
UP IN
~ FS 16 ~

FAVORIT

Memorandum

von ...., den .... 19.... an ....

THE MASTER WITH THE SHARPEST KNIFE IN TOWN

By Stephanie M. Rebonati

There's so much and yet so little to say about the 33-year-old artist Francisca Silva. So much because her work is a garish fusion of poetry, sculpture, painting, drawing, textiles and tattoos. So little because she doesn't like talking about herself or her work. "I could spout sentimental nonsense," she says, "but I don't want to kill my art with words."

Francisca Silva is a tough girl, a macho, a lesbian. She was born to Chilean refugees in Ticino in 1984, went to school in Italy, studied fine arts in Zürich, moved to Berlin in 2012 and returned to Switzerland in 2015, only to leave again two years later. She is now based in Brooklyn. Short and round, her body is an ever-evolving work of art in and of itself: she wears "jewelry", as she calls her tattoos, on her neck, arms, legs, belly and head, most of which she draws and inks herself. A sea of clouds, an axe, a dolphin, a naked doll. A question in quivering letters: "Are you going to break my heart?"

FAVORIT

Memorandum

von ....

.................., den .... 19...

an ....

Francisca Silva tattoos others, too. In tattoo studios and artist-run spaces, at performances, exhibition openings and readings everywhere from Lugano to Berlin, from Seoul to Chicago and New York. Kitted out with her ink and iron, she calls herself “Fra Macho”. “Macho” is also the name of her one-woman publishing house, and the word is indelibly inked into her left thigh as well.

“Macho” sums up one of the cycles that reflect her view of herself as an artist, cycles and phases that have already given rise to a dense and multi-faceted oeuvre. But her self-styled machismo and tattoos are only one facet of her work. Equally important and impressive are her extravagantly designed walk-through cardboard installations, the first of which was publicly displayed in 2012 at the Helmhaus in Zürich. One such installation comprises a cave, painted white on the outside, with an eclectic and colorful collage of self-portraits, drawings, cut-outs and vagina-shaped sculptures on the inside. It’s called “This Is Not a Love Story”. And yet that’s precisely what Silva’s art is: an expression of her ambivalent love story with the folly and beauty of this world. In 2013 she constructed an even bigger and more colorful installation at the Kunstmuseum Baselland with an even more cryptic title: “Makumba-Temple of YOLO” (“YOLO” as in “you only live once”). And it just happened to trigger the start of a new cycle in Basel.

FAVORIT

Memorandum

von .... an ....

...., den .... 19 ....

Brushed or sprayed on with a mere flick of the wrist, Silva's short curves of color were christened "Würmchen" and first publicly exhibited in 2014 at Bern's Stadtgalerie. A sea of little worms swimming towards the viewer. Multi-colored and executed on various media, including canvasses and large bed sheets trimmed with triangles of Caribbean batik fabric, T-shirts dangling from the ceiling on heavy metal chains, sweatshirts and caps. The exhibition was titled "Francisca Silva". "The worms are a joke," she said at the time with a grin on her earnest face.

The worms were followed by something that wasn't merely another cycle, but another genre altogether: Silva started writing. And she called her word combinations "poetry". Not sayings or slogans, but "poetry", as though the very word were the most precious thing in the world. Silva's poetry is dead serious. Though not humorless. Sexy, maybe. Mischievous, most likely. Unfiltered and unrefined, childlike, one might say, but definitely not childish.

FAVORIT

Memorandum

von .... an ....

....

.............................., den.............................19.........

In 2015, in her first solo show at Zürich's Herrmann Germann Contemporary gallery, Silva's large painted sheets of unframed canvas, suspended from the ceiling, became studies in pain. Sublime pain spreading as silently as fog when something comes to an end. The paintings were as loud as ever, to be sure, the letters sharp and clear, the colors sprayed on in lavish sweeping gestures. And yet their content weighed heavy. They hung innocently from the ceiling, in a staggered arrangement spread out liberally in the exhibition space, making showgoers feel they'd wandered into a multicolored labyrinth.

I'M THE CODE BETWEEN YOUR LEGS
IF IT'S NOT YOU / I GO HOME
CAN'T FEEL

The handwritten words on linen were the result of a struggle that Silva had waged with herself. She struggled to drive out demons. And she won. She left the battlefield victorious, even calling herself "Samurai" for a while, and tattooed the words "POET OF YOUR HEART" on her neck. For she had discovered words, language.

FAVORIT

Memorandum

von .... an ....

............, den............ 19......

She'd already been writing for some time, but this was the first time she made her fragile and yet brutal lines public. She tore the pain out of her soul—and wrapped it in rap.

I'M THE MASTER WITH THE SHARPEST KNIFE IN TOWN
I GOT YOUR SEX UNDER MY BEAT
BIG FRA GIVES IT TO YOU FRESH

She banned booze and drugs from her life and gave herself another indelible badge, this time in black ink on her right hand: "Clean & Sober". Since then the young artist has been subtly winding her way in English, German and Spanish through the stormy seas of an ambivalent soul in the throes of courting, conquest and consummation. This is her game and she loves it. Especially since detoxing back to lucidity.

FAVORIT

Memorandum

von ...... an ......

......, den ...... 19......

BABY WE SHOULD BE A POEM IN YOUR BED
MEET ME AT THE BOTTOM OF THAT SWEET SWEET SONG
AND YOUR VOICE PRETTY GIRL LICKS MY HEART

Silva has a hard time explaining herself. Art simply happens, she says. Maybe it says nothing at all. Maybe it's just a lifestyle, a business, a quest, a path. The fact is: she can't help it. Ever since she began thinking for herself she's been painting and making things. This is her attempt to understand the world. "I might be a 33-year-old woman who wants to be 25, if not 20, forever," she once said. "YOLO forever." She often describes what she does, as well as herself and the world in general, as "one big joke with plenty of pathos".

It's hard to determine whether these eye-catching statements are expressions of belated teenage defiance or unaffected truths enunciated with brutal earnestness. Truths about a lesbian artist in a heteronormative society who's striving for a life exclusively devoted to art. Who worked for three years at a beverage supplier's depot in order to come to grips with her life. In order to stay clean, to lead a normal everyday existence, to get far away

FAVORIT

Memorandum

von ....

an ....

...., den .... 19 ....

from art … only in order to rediscover it—in the middle of a storm. Who refuses to justify her sexuality, her flirtation with commercialism, or her primitive working methods. Who stands there and says to the world: "Here I am and I have something to say." And says it loud and clear, in all caps:

FROM NOW ON THE TREMENDOUS PAIN OF MY SOUL
IS GONNA BE THE SUNSHINE ON MY FACE

Stephanie M. Rebonati is a New York-based editor for Edition Patrick Frey and a freelance writer on art and culture.

FAVORIT

Memorandum

von ....
, den .... 19....

an ....

Francisca Silva
25 Memoranden

All artwork: Francisca Silva
Text & copyediting: Stephanie Rebonati
Translation & proofreading: Eric Rosencrantz
Reproductions: Cédric Tournier-Colletta, Atelier Carbon3
Book design: Teo Schifferli
Assistance: Anne Stock

Printed and bound by Druckhaus Köthen
Lithography: DZA Druckerei zu Altenburg GmbH
Paper for text: Lessebo Smooth Ivory, 115 g/m²
Cover: Munken Print White, 150 g/m²
Font: Times New Roman

First edition: Edition Patrick Frey, 2017
Print run: 700 copies
ISBN 978-3-906803-45-6
Printed in Germany

Edition Patrick Frey, Limmatstrasse 268, CH-8005 Zürich
www.editionpatrickfrey.com
mail@editionpatrickfrey.ch

Special thanks to:
La mammina siempre!
Steph!
Bubi!
Mary en Seúl!
And my Wife for being so cool to know this was for her.

FAVORIT

Memorandum

von ....

an ....

.............................., den .... 19......

Distribution

Switzerland:
AVA Verlagsauslieferung, CH – Affoltern am Albis
ava.ch

Germany, Austria:
GVA Gemeinsame Verlagsauslieferung, D – Göttingen
gva-verlage.de

France, Luxembourg, Belgium:
Les presses du réel, F – Dijon
lespressesdureel.com

United Kingdom:
Antenne Books, GB – London
antennebooks.com

Japan:
twelvebooks, JP – Tokyo
twelve-books.com

United States:
RAM publications + distribution, USA – Santa Monica
rampub.com

Australia, New Zealand:
Perimeter Distribution, AU – Melbourne
perimeterdistribution.com

Rest of the world:
Edition Patrick Frey, CH – Zürich
editionpatrickfrey.com

FAVORIT